What Do I Need?

The basics of being set free.

From the book "What Do I Want?"

A Booklet by

Diane C. Shore

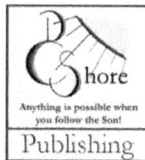

DCShore Publishing
dcshorepublishing.com
Copyright © 2019 Diane C. Shore

1.12

ISBN-13: 978-1732678545

WHAT DO I WANT?
AVAILABLE IN PAPERBACK AND KINDLE

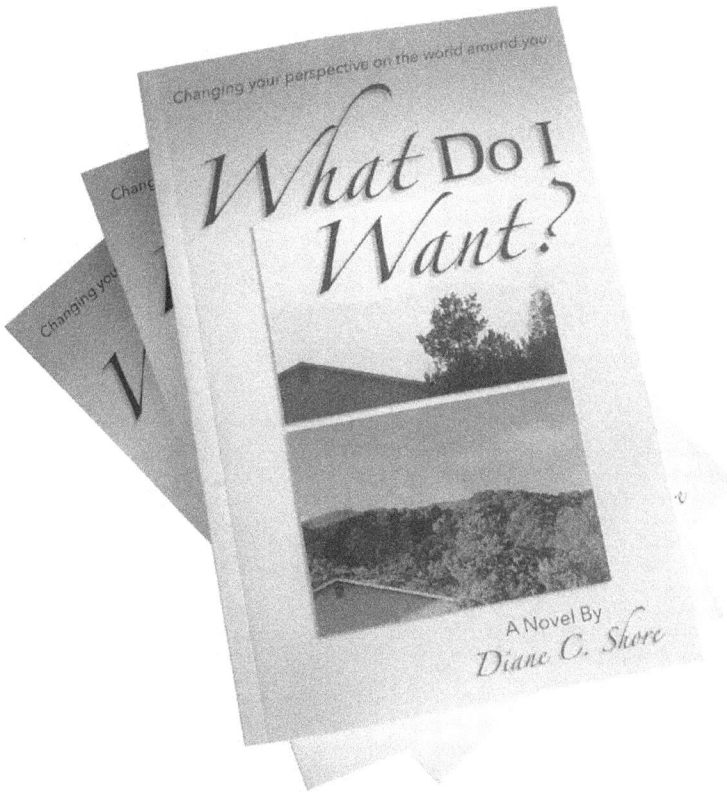

CONTENTS

FINDING YOUR FREEDOM!   Pg # 1

PROLOGUE   Pg # 3

1 WHERE AM I TODAY?   Pg # 5

2 DO I NEED HELP?   Pg # 9

3 WHERE DO I START?   Pg #13

4 WHERE DID I GET HUNG UP?   Pg #17

5 WHAT DO I NEED TO LET GO OF?   Pg #21

6 AM I COMMITTED TO LIVING FREE?   Pg #25

7 HOW DO I FINISH WELL?   Pg #29

8 HOW DOES THIS LOOK IN MY EVERY DAY?   Pg #33

9 IS PHYSICAL HEALING PART OF THE PACKAGE?   Pg #37

10 WHAT CAN I DO EACH DAY FOR PROTECTION?   Pg #43

11 SALVATION, DELIVERANCE AND   Pg #47
    THE GREAT COMMISSION

12 WHAT DOES DEMONIZATION LOOK LIKE?   Pg #51

13 WHERE DO I GO FROM HERE?   Pg #55

14 SUMMARY AND PRAYERS   Pg #59

15 SCRIPTUURE SUGGESTIONS   Pg #65

FINDING YOUR FREEDOM!

The Spirit of the Sovereign Lord is on me,
because the Lord has anointed me
to proclaim good news to the poor.
He has sent me to bind up the brokenhearted,
to proclaim freedom for the captives.
And release from darkness for the prisoners.

Isaiah 61:1

Your quest for Freedom starts with submission to Jesus Christ as Lord and Savior. Submission, forgiveness, repentance, and restitution are the first steps toward healing and deliverance. If you have never prayed a prayer of salvation, let today be the day! The angels in Heaven rejoice when even one sinner repents and is saved!

"Father, I come to You today to give You my heart, broken as it might be. I ask for Your forgiveness for my sins, admitting to You that I have done many things that are probably an offense to You. I thank You for sending Your One and only Son, Jesus, to die for my sins. I believe Jesus rose again on the third day conquering sin and death. I want to live in the freedom He died to give me. I want to live forever in Your heavenly Kingdom with You. Wash me with Your cleansing blood, Jesus. Make me new again. Save my soul for all of eternity. Amen."

This is the most important prayer you can ever pray. What follows are the many gifts and blessings that come with a renewed life in Christ.

Diane C. Shore

PROLOGUE

This booklet can be used alone, or in conjunction with the book, "What Do I Want." The book is PACKED with information and prayers that can later be hard to locate. This booklet can be a handy reference guide. If you have already read the book, then I don't need to give you a "spoiler alert" with what is contained in here. If you haven't, then you have been "alerted."

Inner healing and deliverance ministries heal the wounds where Satan found an entrance into our lives, and tell Satan he has to GO, NOW! Putting Satan in his place is Biblical. Jesus did it, and He taught us to do it as He modeled it in the Gospels. Walking in this authority is living in the freedom Jesus died to give us. It is bold, and it is TRUE!

In the beginning, all of this can seem a bit overwhelming. But if we are willing to search for the freedom that comes with healing and deliverance, in the end, it can become so simple we will wonder why we never knew about it before—we will begin to be perplexed as to why so many are resistant to it. I know, because I was there, as were some of my friends who are now experiencing this new freedom in Christ.

In 1 Corinthians 1:18-31, it starts with, *"I know very well how foolish the message of the cross sounds to those who are on the road to destruction. But we who are being saved recognize this message as the very power of God."* And then in verse 23, it says, *"So when we preach that Christ was crucified, the Jews are offended, and the Gentiles say it's all nonsense."* Finishing with verse 31, *"The person who wishes to boast should boast only of what the Lord has done."*

So, here's my prayer for not only the book, but now this booklet...

"Father in Heaven, thank You. I pray this is a work of Your hands, and I will *boast only of what the Lord has done* and give You all the glory You are so deserving of. Some will be *offended*, some will call it all *nonsense*. But my only desire is to serve You, to honor You, and be used as an instrument in Your Kingdom work, putting the enemy in his place. I pray this helps to encourage anyone in bondage, anyone who is wounded, and anyone who is walking in a smoky haze to now move forward in freedom, be healed, and see clearly with all of their focus on Your Son, the Lord Jesus Christ. Amen."

I hope this booklet simplifies what might seem complicated by the lies of the enemy who is only out to steal, kill and destroy God's children. We have been given all the weapons we need to defeat the enemy in the power of Jesus' name. It is important to use each and every one. When we worship, pray, and study the Word of God, we will find that Jesus is everything we will ever need. When we plead the blood of Jesus, there is great power at hand. When we apply anointing oil, there is even more protection provided.

May the abundant life of Jesus Christ be received fully!

1

WHERE AM I TODAY?

Let's start with where you may find yourself on this day. In the book, it's on page 85:

——◆❦❈❦◆——

"I'm just empty of feeling…well, other than frustration, anger, and disappointment. Those are the emotions I seem to run on most days."

"Join the human race, Randy. If we took a poll, there are many who run on those emotions, and some even darker. Talk about an empty gas tank. Don't you wonder what we're all doing on this planet, anyway? What's the point? Why have we been put here? To do what? And why?"

"Those are good questions. Don't tell me you have the answers, because I'm pretty sure I won't believe you."

Eric laughs.

——◆❦❈❦◆——

This is no laughing matter is it? Not to you, not to me, not to anyone because most of us have been there or are still there.

If you were to describe how you're feeling today, what would you write?

_____

_____

_____

_____

Where do these emotions begin? Do they have a clear place of origin? It's hard for most of us to know, but there is Someone who does, the Holy Spirit. Most know about our Father in Heaven, most know about His Son, Jesus Christ, but how many of us know about the Holy Spirit? Let's spend just a bit of time getting to know Him because He is going to be VERY important on this quest for freedom.

He, the Holy Spirit, is the third Person of the Trinity. He is not an "it". He is as much a "He" as the Father and the Son. His role in the Godhead is huge! The Father, we know, sits on the Throne in Heaven. He is the One who sent His One and Only Son to this earth to pay for the sins of all. Jesus, who came to earth, was born as the Son of God through Mary, died on the Cross, rose again, and is now seated at the right hand of the Father in Heaven. He intercedes for us. He is our Advocate. When the Father sees us, those who have given our lives to Jesus as our Savior, He no longer sees our sins— the Father sees His perfect Son, the spotless Lamb of God. Our sins have been washed away by Jesus' blood—we have been cleansed and been made new and readied for Heaven when our time comes.

The role of the Holy Spirit is to live within each believer after we have given our hearts to Jesus. Jesus ascended back into Heaven after His resurrection and spending 40 days on this earth showing everyone He truly had risen from the dead. He told the disciples not to leave Jerusalem until they received the Gift His Father would be sending them. That Gift is the Holy Spirit. Apart from Jesus, we can do nothing. But we are never apart from Him because the Holy Spirit now dwells within us. He is our Comforter, our Counselor, our Helper, our Guide, and everything we will ever need to live the victorious Christian life!

But do we? That's an important question to ask ourselves.

NOTES:

2

DO I NEED HELP?

Let's move on now to how Linda, in the book on page 57, is coming to terms with her own struggles:

———◆◆❀◆◆———

"I might as well tell you, I left my husband last night. The return home wasn't good, and I'm staying with my sister now, not knowing really what's in store for my future."

"Oh. Wow. That was a difficult return home for sure. I'm really sorry to hear it," Trisha says, comfortingly.

"Thanks." After a few moments of silence, I can tell Trisha is not wanting to rush me. I know I need to say something. "That's why I wanted to call you instead of text. I think…I know, I need some help. I'm not sure what that will look like, but…I don't really know what to say. Just that, I guess. I need help."

"That's a very good place to start, Linda."

———◆◆❀◆◆———

And it is! We all have to start the healing journey somewhere. When we admit that we need help, it opens up the possibility to find that help. In this story, Trisha is going to be a guide to help Linda find healing. (I told you, "spoiler alert." If you would rather read the whole story first, you can stop here and come back when you are done.)

Linda and Randy are married. They are having problems, like all married couples do in one form or another. Both need healing, and both need intentional prayers that will lead them toward the freedom that Jesus died to give them. They are both Christians in this story. But their walk with Jesus has been distant, at best. They just aren't finding the joy that they hear about twice a year when they attend church on Christmas and Easter. They wonder if the smiles that others wear in the church are even real?

How are your smiles on this day? Are they real? Or are you just trying to "fit in" when you attend church? Are you ready to say, "I need help?"

_____

_____

_____

_____

Needing help is not shameful. Jesus came to give us that very help. His Father sent the Helper from Heaven to live inside of us each day. Needing Jesus is not showing weakness; it is showing strength…admitting the problem, and going after the solution. It's not running away scared; it's running to the Source of our Peace and Hope. What are our other choices? If you have read the book, you've seen the choices that Randy makes. I won't give them away just yet. And you will see the choices Linda is making. You will probably relate to some, if not a lot of them. And that is good, because even though the book is a work of fiction, it has so much real life in it that it will probably make you uncomfortable at times. When getting to the root of things, digging deep, and finding out what's hurting, can…well, hurt. But some pain is revealing, showing us where restoration is needed in our lives. Our Father in Heaven knows what's needed. He sees our past and our future. The Holy Spirit will reveal what's come through previous generations into our lives that needs to have a stop put to it in our generation. There may even be things that we, or past relatives, have been involved in that opened the door to darkness through curses or occult activity like Ouija boards, palm readers, seances, etc… God knows all, and wants to free us from it all, if we will only seek His face, and ask.

The pain that Jesus endured on the Cross for us brought us everything we need to live full and abundant lives on this day. Let's stop right here and pray:

"Father, thank You for sending Your Son, Jesus, to this world. Thank You, Jesus, for the pain You endured on the Cross for us. You went, willingly, even though as You said in Matthew 26:53,54 *'Don't you realize that I could ask my Father for thousands of angels to protect us, and he would send them instantly? But if I did, how would the Scriptures be fulfilled that describe what must happen now?'* You could have skipped it all, Jesus. But You didn't. You suffered for us, and we want to live in the freedom Your suffering provided. Thank You, Jesus. We appreciate all You have done for us. Mold us. Shape us. Guide us. In Your Name we pray. Amen."

NOTES:

3

WHERE DO I START?

Freedom starts with forgiveness. It did on the Cross, and it still does to this day. Jesus said, *"Father, forgive them, for they do not know what they are doing."* (Luke 23:34) Can we say the same? Many times, we don't want to forgive, do we? But we MUST. This is vital! Listen in on what Trisha is telling Linda on page 76:

———✦———

"I know this is a hard step. But it is an important first one. This is not saying that what they did didn't hurt you or that it wasn't terrible. This isn't even about how you feel about it or them. This is about giving all of that to God to deal with and letting Him heal your memories and feelings over time, however long it takes. This is a decision you are making, a choice, one that will begin to set you free. This is for you, not them. They won't even know it is happening. But your heart, soul, mind, and spirit will. Forgiveness will be pivotal in setting *you* free."

"Uh…I don't know. This makes me fidgety just thinking about it. I guess I can start with Randy, huh?"

"Randy would be a good place to start, of course. Remember, this doesn't mean you have to run right over there and repair your marriage. This is about repairing your damaged heart…putting your own oxygen mask on first. Let God take care of the rest," Trisha explains.

———✦———

Forgiveness is hard. But do you know what is harder? Unforgiveness. The ripple effect of unforgiveness not only damages your own heart, it damages every relationship you have in life. You may not think so, but if you were to ask others around you, and if they were to be really honest with you, you would see that it is true. Unforgiveness is something we wear, and it is heavy, and it is very ugly…sorry to say.

Are you willing to give forgiveness a try? Linda put Randy first on her list. Who would you like to put on yours? List their name, and their offense, if only in your mind, and then offer them forgiveness. Ask God to help you. He will. And then let Him handle it. He will. And He will begin to heal your heart in amazing ways.

I choose to forgive _____ for _____.

I choose to forgive _____ for _____.

And now, begin another list, either on paper, or in your own head, for yourself. Your Father in Heaven wants to forgive you also. Jesus died on the Cross for you!

Father, please forgive me for _____. I'm so very sorry. I agree with Your Word that speaks against this, and I choose to align my life and my thoughts with Your Truth.

Father, please forgive me for _____. I'm so very sorry. I agree with Your Word that speaks against this, and I choose to align my life and my thoughts with Your Truth.

And now, this is VERY IMPORTANT, receive the forgiveness that Jesus died to give you! He removes our sins from us as far as the east is from the west and remembers them no more. So, neither should we. We aren't more forgiven if we punish ourselves for another day, week, year, or decade. That does no good, it only keeps our sins weighing heavy on us. Our Father in Heaven sees us cleansed with the blood of His Son. Let's live in that cleanness and breathe free!

Repentance is all part of this, and it is included above when we turn from our sins and desire to live our life in accordance with God's Word. Remorse is not repentance. We can be sorry for something, but still choose to live that way. We must repent to be set free. This doesn't mean we will never sin again—this means we choose not to practice that sin over and over thinking we can live however we want. Repentance is agreeing with God's Word and aligning our life, day by day, with that Truth. Following that agreement, the turning away from the sinful temptation is the fruit that comes from repentance.

Restitution is another part of being set free. If we owe something to someone, let's pay them back. Let's make it good! We can live free of the weight of that.

NOTES:

4

WHERE DID I GET HUNG UP?

When Judas betrayed Jesus for thirty pieces of silver, he knew he had done wrong. He wanted to return the money, but it could not be legally taken back. They bought a place called Potter's Field with it. It was called that because of the clay located there. This is where Judas went and hung himself after his sin of betraying Jesus. What a ghastly ending to what could have been a life as an Apostle. He was one of the 12 chosen. But he chose otherwise…with the help of Satan.

What has Satan done in your life that's tempting you to choose something other than the life of purity, hope, love, and serving the King of kings? The enemy inflicts us all somewhere along the way. But if we can identify where that wounding happened, and what came with it, we can have it healed by the stripes of our Lord and Savior, and we can move on from there as a new creation in Christ.

You may be saying, I don't know what it is that has me in bondage…could it be the day I was bullied in school? What about the day I was fired from that job? Or the Christmas when I felt slighted by the gifts my brother got compared to mine? Some have suffered terribly at the hands of another with all kinds of abuse, through no fault of their own. Whatever it was, it was an opportunity for the enemy, Satan, to make his entrance into our lives. He looks at those times as "open doors" to come in and steal, kill, and destroy the life we have been blessed with. His lies become strongholds that we need to tear down and throw out. There's Good News in all of this! Jesus made a way for us to not only be healed from the wounds, but to also evict the "thief" who has come to do such damage. He doesn't belong in our "home." He's an invader. We can kick him out and lock the door!

Let's listen in as Linda shares on page 78 about a time in her life when the enemy found an entrance:

"Holy Spirit, help Linda to think back, and recall something that has caused her maybe, to be troubled in her life. Bring to her something that needs Your healing touch today. Show her if it was a person, a trauma, maybe there was some verbal or physical abuse, an incident with Randy? Is it something that she's not proud of that she did? Whatever it is, bring that darkness into the light, Lord Jesus. I'm going to give you some time now Linda, no rush."

(After some minutes have passed, Linda says this.)

"It's a sad memory. The day my grandma died, and I got the call…"

"Okay. That's a good place to start. Grief is hard. We're going to pray together and for you about that now. Holy Spirit, thank You for revealing this painful time in Linda's life. There's still hurt that hasn't been resolved it seems, but You would like to heal this wound in Linda. Thank You for that. And if any darkness pierced Linda's soul that day, causing her to be in bondage, then we will be seeking Your removal of that, also. It has no place in your life, Linda."

The Holy Spirit reveals things that are buried deep inside if we will ask Him, wait, listen, and then process the things He wants us to know. Many times, what is revealed to us will seem insignificant, but it's not. A wound is a wound, and we should spend time there allowing God to heal it in a way that only He can. These wounds will seem painful at first, but when we finish going through the healing process, it will then be an old scar…something we will remember but that no longer causes us pain.

Let's pray:

"Father in Heaven, I know You know me as no other. You know every hair that You placed on my head. You know when a sparrow falls from the sky. You have seen every day that I have lived, and even when I was still in my mother's womb, You knew me. Help me on this day, Holy Spirit, to know what it is You see as a need in me that could use Your healing touch. Reveal it to me, bring it into the light of Your love, and cleanse it of the infection that has set in. I give it to You today, and anything associated with it that has been causing me harm. Pour Your healing love into this wound. I release it all to You today. In the powerful name of Jesus, Amen."

NOTES:

5

WHAT DO I NEED TO LET GO OF?

When we come to our Father with open hands, letting go of the things that lie behind, we are free to move forward into what He has for us in the future. We can find joy…true joy.

Linda and Randy, in this story, have lots of history together. They have been married a good many years, they have two children, and they are expecting their first grandchild. It seems that life should be good with a nice home, two good jobs, and their health. But it isn't. It's full of strife, anger, bitterness, addictions, and all the things that many of us deal with in life. And like most of us, they could remain that way not knowing what's available through the atoning blood of Jesus. Thankfully, God is bringing people into their lives who can help. There are people that God can bring into your life, too. When you admit you need help, when you go looking for it, and praying for it, God provides in amazing ways. It's hard at first, it can be scary, but it's well worth it in the end.

Let's take another look at where Randy is in this process on page 84:

One night while flipping through my phone, I see Eric's name. I haven't given him a second thought. I've really had no interest. Do I now? I fiddle with my phone awhile, stalling. I don't really want to call him. It's too weird. And I don't really want to talk to anyone about my life. But for some strange reason, I push his number. He answers…

"Eric here. What's up?" he says.

"Hi. It's Randy. You called me a few weeks back."

"Hi, Randy. How ya doin'?"

"Uh, I don't know. I don't even know why I'm calling you. I really didn't mean to," I stammer out the words.

"Oh. Well, now that you did, want to talk?" he asks without a hint of hesitation.

———————

Can you see yourself in this scenario? That first phone call seems so hard to make. What will I say? How will they respond? It's too scary! But we will see as this story unfolds, it can be a very good thing.

Is there someone you should try calling today? Is there someone God has placed in your life to help you find healing and restoration?

The Bible says that when we are called into the courts, the Holy Spirit will give us the words we need. I have found that this is true throughout all of life. When we don't know what to say, if we will just make the attempt, the Holy Spirit will meet us right there. He will help us through it. Remember, that's His job…He's our Helper! We just need to let go of our pride and reach out with open hands to the gift of freedom the Father is offering us. Satan's job is to keep us bound, God's promise is to set us free.

Randy is doing that here, and Linda has done it with Trisha. Listen in as the Holy Spirit reveals things that Linda's soul has been holding onto after her grandma's shocking death. When calling on the name of the Lord Jesus, so many things that have been holding us in bondage can be gotten rid of.

Page 79 of the book:

Trisha then asks me to be still as she starts in with a firm voice saying, "I command all the shock, loneliness and whatever else pierced Linda's soul on that day to go right now in Jesus' name. I command any dark spirit that was associated with this, to this memory, and any memory of family dysfunction during that time to be healed also. We thank You, Lord Jesus, for healing Linda in this area. Jesus, You bind up the brokenhearted. I declare that the enemy can never cause Linda anguish over this memory again. She is healed in Your powerful name, Lord Jesus."

Words are powerful in the spiritual realm. Satan hears us, and he hates it when we use the name of Jesus as we have been called to for healing and deliverance. Satan doesn't want us to say as Jesus did, *"It is written…"* Being set free in deliverance has all been given such a bad rap by Hollywood. What the Bible calls us to do is so very different. It is loving, and it is kind. It can get intense at times, but not in a bad way. As one person put it, it's like a "spiritual detox."

NOTES:

6

AM I COMMITTED TO LIVING FREE?

When a house is swept clean, it takes work to keep it that way. We do our dishes daily, we clean our houses weekly, we mow our lawn when needed. Living free takes maintenance also. It takes commitment to time in the Word, time with other believers, time in prayer (perhaps with fasting), and focus on the things that are right, true, and worthy of praise. The enemy will know if we're serious about this. Not that there won't be setbacks…there will be. Sometimes a new wound will be revealed. But we can know now how to deal with it. Many times the enemy will continue to knock on our door—now we can know who's there and what they want. But sometimes we still walk to the door and open it…maybe even just a crack. This allows the enemy room to operate in our lives again…giving him a "foothold"—a space that he can inhabit. If we do this, we will need to kick him out again! But one step back doesn't need to keep us from taking another two steps forward.

Randy and Linda are working through many things in the book. As in life, they have different challenges. They want different things. But when our focus is on Jesus, relationships are able to function in the way that God designed them. Not perfectly, but under the guidance of a perfect Savior. Both Randy and Linda show us what it looks like to be committed to restoration, or not. They walk through this battle being taught how to use all the weapons that we have been given. The war has been won. Jesus is the Victor, as are we. But until we hear the final, *final* words, "It is finished," we will still be on this earth struggling. That's not to be a downer, that's just to be real. When we get real, we can heal. If we are going to live in a false reality, we are going to be playing in the devil's playground. And it can be addicting! Take a look at what happens on page 216 of the book:

"Eric, ummm, this isn't something I wanted to be doing. It started off with a 'hello' and quickly went where I never wanted it to. But truth be told, I thought about it most of the night afterward, and she is supposed to get ahold of me again tonight. I don't even know how to say, 'No' to it. Because, honestly, I want to do it." I hated being so blunt with Eric.

We do have to ask ourselves, "What Do I Want?" If we can't even be honest with ourselves, if we are just fooling ourselves like the Bible talks about, then let's ask the Holy Spirit for help, once again. That is why He is there! Really, we are not bothering Him. And God already knows what we're going to ask before we ask it. Yes! He does! And He's just waiting for us…lovingly, patiently, and kindly, waiting for us to come to our senses. The enemy makes no sense. The enemy is about confusion, and chaos. God is a God of order— so if things are out of order in our lives, we are probably out of God's will. This is not to say life will be perfect and without troubles. The Bible is clear that we will have trouble. But if we go to our Father each day asking for His guidance and help, we will find amazing answers being given to us.

In Revelation it says, *"Those who are willing to hear, should listen, and understand what the Spirit is saying to the churches."* God wants to talk to us, and He wants us to listen to Him and obey Him. Otherwise, as it says in James 1, *"…it is like glancing at your face in the mirror. You see yourself, walk away, and forget what you look like."* What good does that do?

Let's keep looking steadily into the Truth that's been given to set us free and we will see amazing results. Sadly, too many are walking around in a smoky haze and not even knowing that there are clear blue skies available to those of us who call Jesus Savior and Lord.

If you want a visual of this, take a look at the cover of this book. On the cover of the book, "What Do I Want," you will see two photos. These are the same scene, taken four days apart. One is a picture of a clear blue sky, the other is a picture of a smoke-filled sky. How many of us are living in this toxicity? Jesus died for so much more than that!

NOTES:

7

HOW DO I FINISH WELL?

Randy and Linda's story is not all that different from each one of ours. Yes, the names, the places, and the incidents are different…but we are all doing life here on planet earth. We are all challenged and tempted. We have all been wounded. We all need love. And ultimately, I believe we all want to live free. How blessed we are to live in America. Have you ever thought about what your life would be like had you been born in another country? In another era? Why has God placed you here for just such a time as this? I know I am very grateful.

When finding healing, when being delivered and set free from so much that has plagued us too many days of our lives, we will begin on a whole new journey…one that can give us a new perspective on the world around us. Just as our best deeds are filthy rags to our perfect Father in Heaven, so our best view of things here is skewed by afflictions we have no idea are even affecting us. When we think we know the Truth, we can be shocked to find out we don't. When we think we know what someone said, or did, we can be surprised to find out it is very different than that. When we are delivered from the spirit of fear, or anger, or greed, we can suddenly see and feel things in a whole new way. Many times, we are then able to see it from the other person's perspective and it makes us more loving, and kind concerning the things they are dealing with. We can start to realize that the reason that guy is grumpy, the reason that woman is crying, the reason that person said those hurting words is because they are so wounded; they know no other way of being. And only by putting our "oxygen mask" on first can we even begin to help another. Otherwise we truly are the blind trying to lead the blind.

This little booklet in no way can cover every aspect of what the full novel "What Do I Want" covers in the more than 111,000 words it contains. But I hope that what I'm sharing here will help wet your appetitive for the full story. As I reveal what is found on page 270, I warn you, it is a huge spoiler alert! But with it, I hope you will know that their story, your story, can be about restoration and hope and love. It can be about Jesus, and all He died to give us. It can be about how much our Father in Heaven loves us, and how the Holy Spirit is so instrumental in all of it. When we get to know the Spirit that lives inside of us, we can truly discern what is coming against us, what needs to go in our lives, and where healing can be found on a daily basis.

This is not a one-time thing. This is a daily walk with Jesus. A fun one! An exciting one! An amazing one full of miracles and joy that will astound all of us! Page 270 from the book:

—✦✦✦—

Everything I have learned is spilling over into all the other areas of my life. The Fruit of the Spirit becomes more obvious now. It seems the more I learn to walk in the Light, the more I can love others around me, including my neighbors....

….When I was in my own world and miserable, I thought I was the only one struggling. Now that I've stopped being so focused on myself, I know that this is a hurting world, and people need God's love, as did I. The meaner I was, the meaner I got. It was a vicious circle—probably because I was so guilt ridden over it all. But Eric clearly explained that Jesus not only makes us nicer through the power of the Holy Spirit, He takes that guilt away through Jesus' death on the Cross. Satan has been shackled, not us.

If you haven't figured it out, this story has a happy ending. Yours can, too. Not because your life will be perfect, but because with Jesus we have the Victory. And learning to walk in that Victory every day can leave us content whether we have little or much. When we see the enemy defeated on a daily basis—and he will come at us almost every day—we are really beginning to experience the true authority that Jesus died to give us. He gave the keys of the Kingdom of Heaven back to us that Adam and Eve gave away. Yes, Jesus returned them to Peter in Matthew 16:19. Now we just need to learn how to use them to unlock our freedom!

If you haven't read the book, this is giving you a good glimpse of what it contains. Some, who went into it hesitantly, came out KNOWING that the Truth can truly set us free!

"Father, You are good. You provide. You are amazing. Thank You for sending Jesus to save us. Now, help us continue to walk in that saving grace until we meet You face to face. We love You and appreciate You. We give You all the praise and glory forever and ever. In Jesus' name. Amen."

NOTES:

8

HOW DOES THIS LOOK IN MY EVERY DAY?

Some are of the mistaken impression that inner healing and deliverance are a one-time, fix-it-all experience. Why do I keep emphasizing this point? Because it's a lie! Yes, an intense session of prayer with others can accomplish wonderful results, but daily maintenance on our own is vital. Continued growth is important. Follow-up prayers can be important. We don't teach a baby how to crawl and leave the baby to crawl around the rest of its life. Months later we take their hands and teach them how to walk…we encourage them to put one foot in front of the other. When they fall, we teach them how to get up, and walk some more. This is very similar. There is a learning to "walk" in the freedom. The enemy will want us to fall, but the falling is not a sin. The laying on the floor in the mud and mire is where we will get messed up. We are called to submit to God. To humble ourselves before Him. He will then lift us up.

"Pride goes before destruction, a haughty spirit before a fall."
Proverbs 16:18

Daily practice doesn't make for perfection, but it surely helps. Doctors practice medicine, and Christians should practice Christianity. Practice praying for yourself and others. Practice reading the Word every day until it becomes a habit. Practice thinking things that are good and worthy of praise, talked about in Philippians 4:8. Even if we think we are good at something, practicing makes it even better. It's no different with our faith. Why do we even think we can say "Yes" to Jesus, and then continue to live as we did before? Then we grow disappointed with God and the promises He has given us, many times, and it's merely because we haven't learned to live fully in them. This is a life-long process. Let's not get frustrated along the way and give up. Let's keep on until we meet Jesus face to face!

Also, we have the Armor of God for protection. What is that exactly? And how do we put it on? The Armor is talked about in Ephesians 6:10-18. There are six, no seven, pieces that we have been given which are vital to our earthly life of abundancy. The *Belt of Truth* protects us from the lies of the enemy. The *Breastplate of Righteousness* protects our hearts. The *Shoes of Peace* go with us wherever we go. The *Shield of Faith* protects us from the fiery arrows that come at us each day. The *Helmet of Salvation* protects our minds. The *Sword of the Spirit* is the Word of God, cutting between soul and spirit. And the seventh piece you can read about below taken from page 117 of the book:

"And after going through the armor of God, after putting on the six pieces and wielding your sword, move into the seventh piece of armor which is prayer. It is SO powerful! I have heard it called 'God's intercontinental ballistic missile.'"

This Armor comes by surrendering our heart to Jesus, daily time in the Word, believing what we are reading, and putting it into practice. Randy has a request on page 267 of "What Do I Want," as he is realizing his need for all of what Eric is teaching him:

———————◆⊰⧉⊱◆———————

"Can we practice what that will look like for me in my every day? Say I'm driving to work, and I'm frustrated with…well, the guy who spills coffee on me that morning. And then someone tries to cut me off in the parking lot. What would I do, exactly?"

"Good questions, Randy. Okay, identify how the spilled coffee made you feel," Eric responds.

"Well, I was mad. I was thinking he was super clumsy," I answer, remembering that day when it happened.

"Okay. And what about the person who cuts you off in the parking lot?" Eric asks.

"Probably, more anger, and frustration at them being in my way."

"So, you have identified, anger, critical about the clumsy guy, judgmental, frustration, and such, right?" Eric asks.

"Yes."

"Okay, now that you stopped long enough to realize all that has happened and what you are dealing with, call them what they are. There is forgiveness needed, too. Say, 'Spirit of anger, frustration, get out of me now, in the name of the Lord Jesus. I forgive the guy who spilled his coffee on me. I forgive that driver who blocked me. And any judgmental spirit, or critical spirit, you go, too, in Jesus' mighty name. I am a child of God, you have no right to me. Get out now!! Thank You Lord Jesus.' And then breathe that stuff out, and breathe the Holy Spirit in."

"Okay. That seems easy enough, thanks."

———————◆⊰⧉⊱◆———————

Diane C. Shore

NOTES:

9

IS PHYSICAL HEALING PART OF THE PACKAGE?

Jesus wants us to live free. In Hebrews, it says Jesus broke the power of the devil. This includes physical healing. Jesus went about casting out demons, healing the sick and those with leprosy, and raising the dead. It's all there in the pages of Scripture. But many times we aren't fully embracing all that we've been given. Why? Because we don't fully understand it. Honestly, we are a bit scared to even try. Read this account from Linda, when she came to a place in her life where it was worth the risk on page 195:

"Both of you, put your hands on Jordan, and especially one hand on his little head. And I will pray. This is new for me, so bear with me." I feel nervous stepping into this role, having really only seen it done for others, but this is my grandchild… "Okay, let's do this. Father in Heaven, this precious child is so sick, and this fever is consuming his body. The doctors are doing all they can. But we seek Your help right now, in the name of Your Son, Jesus Christ. Just as Jesus healed the little girl in the Bible, we claim that same healing power right now for little Jordan. We tell this fever to GO, in the name of the Lord Jesus, and for all sickness, all weakness, all efforts of the enemy trying to harm Jordan to be stopped immediately. Just like the girl You healed who immediately stood up and walked around. Jordan won't be walking, but we know You can heal his little body and allow him to grow strong and walk one day. I pray that walk will include a strong faith in You as we tell him of this day when You healed him from this fever. We thank You and give You all the praise in advance for what You're doing. In Your mighty name we pray, Jesus. Amen."

When I finished, I just stayed quiet for a time, waiting to hear from Blake and Hannah on the other end as to what was happening…

What will it take for us to come to that place in our lives where chancing looking like a fool will be outweighed by the need before us? Yes, it can feel awkward. We can feel nervous. But WE don't have to do it, Jesus does it for us. All we have to do is pray…with however much faith we have. Faith as small as a mustard seed can move a mountain. Healing comes **by** grace, through faith. We can leave the results to our Father in Heaven.

Linda prayed a more complicated prayer in the book. Ours doesn't have to be long and complicated to see amazing answers. It can be a simple, direct, and intentional prayer like this:

In the name of the Lord Jesus Christ, I command the pain in (name)_____'s knee to GO!

You have no right to be here. (Name)_____ is a child of the living God. GET OUT! NOW!

Then ask the person if the pain is better. If it's gone, then praise Jesus. If it has decreased from an 8 to a 6, go ahead and pray again. Bring the pain level down with repeated prayers, if needed—thanking

Jesus for what He is doing. The words aren't what's important here. What's important is praying in the authority we have been given. And obviously, it has to be tailored to what the specific disease, pain, or illness is: "Headache, go now, in the name of Jesus Christ." "High blood pressure, return to normal as God designed." "Torn meniscus, be healed, and all surrounding muscles be strengthened." Whatever it is, keep it simple, keep it direct, and be bold!

Here's the risk we take…it can be hard to handle if there is no healing. But here's the benefit…the person you are praying for is being loved on by you. You have taken the time to care about what is going on in their life, and are attempting to do something about it to relieve their suffering. Who doesn't want that?

And if you're wondering if you can pray for yourself? You can! And should. This can be a daily habit of cleaning your temple— getting rid of the thieves that are trying to destroy your life. You can tell that headache pain to go away in Jesus' name. Tell the fear to get out in the name of Jesus Christ. Breathe out the darkness, and then breathe in the fullness of the Holy Spirit. Let Him bless you and others with His goodness and light. If the headache persists, it's okay to take something for it. Luke was a doctor. But why not try to relieve suffering using the power in Jesus' name first and foremost?

Physical healing and spiritual deliverance is what we are called to do. Sadly, we aren't really taught about it, and if we are, we are too afraid most times to walk it out. People shy away when they don't see the results of 100 percent healing and/or deliverance—and what a shame. If a person is willing to pray for the sick, and they only see 2 out of 10 people get healed, should they stop? Aren't the two totally blessed because of their obedience to pray? The other eight experience God's love, if nothing else. If you're really nervous, ask the person who is hurting if you can "practice" on them. That takes some of the pressure off. Just say, "Hey, I'm learning about praying for healing. Can I practice on you?" Then they get to be part of the learning process. Laugh, have fun, experiment! Grow together!

It's true, some people don't get healed. But a lot of people do. These healings, seeing the power of God operating in and through lives, confirms the Gospel up close and personal. It makes our relationship with Jesus all the more fun and exciting!

There is a "high" that comes from seeing a person healed, and there is a "low" and uneasiness when it doesn't happen. But we can trust God for it all. God has three answers, *No*, *Yes*, and *Wait*. To be a part of those answers, we have to pray! Otherwise, we aren't living in the full abundance of what Jesus died to give us, and we can be limited in sharing that abundance of Jesus' love with others! By His stripes we have been healed. By His blood we have been cleansed! AMEN!

NOTES:

Diane C. Shore

10

WHAT CAN I DO EACH DAY FOR PROTECTION?

Being healed and delivered of all the dark stuff life has dumped on us can be the easier part. Like we've talked about, living this out day to day is where the commitment really comes in. Being in the Word every day, praying, worshipping, being with others in the Christian faith, etc… These are all the things that we, in the body of Christ, should be doing. The Lord's prayer (see below), is a good place to begin and/or end our day. Jesus taught His disciples this prayer, and it contains our daily "prescription" for a relationship with our Lord. After "spiritual surgery," cutting out the darkness and filling up with the Light of the Holy Spirit, there is spiritual therapy needed to gain strength and endurance in the battles that ensue. Life will get busy again, things will happen, and maintaining good spiritual health is absolutely necessary for continued victories in the battles of every day.

Spiritual Therapy Prescription

Come to God, go through the Lord's Prayer, personalizing it.

Father, in Heaven (Give thanks to Him)

May Your Name be honored (Give praises to Him)

May Your Kingdom come (Talk to Him about how you're looking forward to Jesus' return)

May Your will be done on earth as it is in Heaven (Thank God for His perfect plan in all things)

Give us this day (Thank God for the new day, for the air you breathe, for your health, etc...)

Our daily Bread (Thank God for all He provides for you, food, home, money, car, clothes, people, etc.)

And forgive us our trespasses (Ask God's forgiveness for recent activities, thoughts, words...)

As we forgive those who trespass against us (Forgive those who have harmed you)

Lead us not into temptation (Ask Abba/Daddy for His help in the temptations you face)

And deliver us from evil (Thank Jesus for saving us from the enemy's grip through His death and resurrection)

For Thine is the Kingdom, the power, and the glory forever! Amen

Daily: Choose a Scripture. Write it on a piece of paper and memorize it. Once memorized, move onto a new Scripture.

Putting God's Word into practice:

When the enemy comes against you, tempts you, or lies to you, speak out, **"IT IS WRITTEN,"** and then say a verse from the Bible over and over until the enemy goes away. This is how Jesus battled the enemy in the wilderness. (See Scripture Suggestions in Chapter 15 of this booklet.)

This is a warning given in Scripture:

"When an unclean spirit goes out of a man, he goes through dry places, seeking rest, and finds none. Then he says, 'I will return to my house from which I came.' And when he comes, he finds it empty, swept, and put in order. Then he goes and takes with him seven other spirits more wicked than himself, and they enter and dwell there; and the last state of that man is worse than the first. So shall it also be with this wicked generation." Matthew 12:43-45

This is why spiritual maintenance is so necessary!

If you don't already have a regular time with God, this is a good time to get started. It will keep your "house" (body and mind) filled with the power of the Holy Spirit. It will start your day focused on the things of God and will help you move forward into your future with confidence in who you are in Christ, how much you are loved and cared about, and the good plans God has for your future. Think of the Lord's Prayer as a prescription from the Great Physician, God. It will make you strong mentally and keep you well spiritually. The side effects of neglecting this time with God cause vulnerability to the enemy and his ways, as talked about in the verse above.

This is a minimum. More is better!

Remember, sin, unforgiveness, the occult, and such, are all invitations to the enemy to come back. Keep the door of your heart, and the window of your mind, shut to him. Resist the enemy, he will flee. Don't answer the door when he comes knocking!!

NOTES:

11

SALVATION, DELIVERANCE AND THE GREAT COMMISSION

The Great Commission was given to us by Jesus. *"All authority in heaven and on earth has been given to me. Therefore go and make disciples of all nations, baptizing them in the name of the Father and the Son and the Holy Spirit, and teaching them to obey everything I have commanded you. And surely I am with you always, to the very end of the age."*

What are some of those things we are to obey? Jesus told His disciples in Matthew 10:7-8, *"Go announce to them that the Kingdom of Heaven is near. Heal the sick, raise the dead, cure those with leprosy, and cast out demons. Give as freely as you have received!"*

Who? Us? Yes! Jesus said, *"I tell you the truth, anyone who believes in me will do the same works I have done, and even greater works, because I am going to be with the Father."* John 14:12

Salvation and Freedom Prayer:

Father in Heaven,

I believe Your Son, Jesus, died on the Cross for my sins and rose again from the dead. I confess all my sins, known and unknown, and I'm sorry for them. I renounce them all. I forgive all others as I want You to forgive me. Please forgive me now. I thank You, Father, for the blood of Your Son, Jesus Christ, which cleanses me from all sin.

You redeemed me by Your blood, and I now belong to You, and I want to live for You. I come to You now as my Deliverer. You know my special needs, the things that bind, that torment, that defile, and any unclean spirit. I claim the promise of Your Word. 'Whosoever calls on the name of the Lord shall be delivered." I call upon You now, in the name of the Lord Jesus Christ. Deliver me and set me free. Amen.

NOTES:

Diane C. Shore

12

WHAT DOES DEMONIZATION LOOK LIKE?

Please remember, a Christian cannot be possessed! This is TRUE! But the word used in the Bible is actually "demonized." In Greek it's "Daimonizomai." This means being under the influence or control of an indwelling spirit. If this is still puzzling to you, picture a target, with the "bullseye" being your spirit, sealed with the Holy Spirit. The next ring around that being your soul, and the one around that being your body. You are a child of God. Nothing can separate you from the love of God. But there are "fiery arrows" aimed at you that can spoil your day, wreck your life, wreak havoc in your emotions, and cause pain and anguish in your life, physically and emotionally.

Spiritual Attacks

Once you have submitted your life to Jesus, you are covered and protected by the blood of Christ. This booklet is to help you start dealing with what the enemy has inflicted, and continues to try to shoot/inflict, into your soul and body every day. Jesus has a remedy for all these attacks! It's called direct and intentional prayer! We are supposed to call on the name of Jesus to deliver us—to remove the arrows that have hit us! Jesus is the Great Deliverer. And He wants us to walk in the **authority** that we have been given...the authority He paid such a high price for! Jesus' death on the Cross was intentional. He could have backed down. He could have called on a legion of angels to rescue Him. But He didn't. He went to the Cross willingly so we could live eternally with our Father in Heaven, and also be set free from the ways of the enemy while we're still on this earth.

Let's begin now to be set free by realizing the bondage we are in. Let's recognize that fiery arrows have sunk deep into our soul leaving us in a toxic, smoky haze. Many are walking around thinking they see/feel right, while others may notice the wounding and bleeding going on. It can come out as anger, fear, anxiety, rejection...you name it. Some even know they have a problem, but aren't willing to face it or deal with it.

The blind man knew he was blind. He knew what to ask Jesus for. When Jesus asked him, "What do you want me to do for you?" His answer was direct. "I want to see." Let's honestly ask ourselves, "What do I want?" And answer that with, "I want Jesus as the Lord and Savior of my life." Then we can find Biblical help and healing.

As one person said about all this; "It's time to WAKE UP!" It's so true! The enemy has lulled us into a deep sleep, and we don't even realize it many times. Jesus can wake us out of our slumber and set us free. Understanding this is one of the first steps. Following through with intentional prayers is another step. It can seem scary. But when the steps are done, it is SO WORTH IT! This is not only about you gaining freedom, but then also learning how to help others in the future in praying for their own fiery arrows to be removed. It's about all of God's children finding freedom. It's what we are called to do, and be, as Christians. These "holes" in our life are then able to be filled to over-flowing with the Holy Spirit...healing what once was wounded.

New Found Freedom

Here are some comments from those who have experienced this new-found freedom:

"It is so quiet! The voices are gone! Is this what peace feels like?"

"The guilt I have lived in for the past 12 years is gone!"

"I came in with pain and a cloudy head. I left with a clear head and relief of pain. There is such a sense of freedom."

"It feels like a weight has been lifted off of me."

NOTES:

Diane C. Shore

13

WHERE DO I GO FROM HERE?

This is not going to fix everything in your life with one "application." Like I said, we don't just do our dishes once and then never again. The dirty dishes will stack up if we don't attend to them frequently. The alternative to not taking care of what is going on in the daily battles we face, is doing life without experiencing the freedom Jesus died and rose again to give us. Where does that take us emotionally, physically, and spiritually? Look around you, and you will see… Many true believers are hurting and lost and needing to learn to live in the promises of Jesus. Jesus has gone ahead to prepare a place for us in Heaven. He is returning soon to take us to the Father. Until then, many of us are here…working out our salvation with fear and trembling, while still needing to understand the power provided for us in the Good News of Jesus Christ.

We have the opportunity to be set free. But the choice is ours to make. Finding help with someone else, in the beginning, is good. But our greatest Source of Help is Jesus. The power is in *His* name. When we call on Jesus and listen to the Holy Spirit guide and direct us on the path of healing and deliverance, we can walk out of the smoky, toxic haze into the clear blue sky of freedom.

If you "fear" the darkness that has left you will come back, that is not an unreasonable fear. It wants to come back. So, first cast out the spirit of fear, and then know that the enemy will come "knocking." It is a fact. But now, I'm reminding you again, you know who is at the door, and what they want. DON'T ANSWER IT! Tell them to GO AWAY! That Jesus lives here, that He reigns supreme, and that they are not wanted! Tell them you have been set free by the Great I AM!

When you know what you want, you can go after it with the authority we have been given through Jesus Christ our King!

If you feel uncomfortable about this, you can simply start by putting your own "oxygen mask" on first in the privacy of your home. Try it out with these simple and direct prayers below and watch what happens.

I command the spirit of _____ to GET OUT in the name of the Lord Jesus Christ!!

You have no right to me, I am a child of the living God. You have to leave NOW! GO! GO! GO!

After taking this authority, breathe out the darkness a few times, and then breathe in the Light of the Holy Spirit. Breathe in deep, filling those empty places with God.

If you are feeling sick, or in pain, you can also command the enemy to leave, the pain to go, by praying for yourself just as we talked about praying for others:

I command the pain in my _____ to GO, in the mighty name of the Lord Jesus! I tell all infection, inflammation, etc…to be healed in the name of Jesus Christ— the One and only Son of the Living God! By His stripes I have been healed!

Will all your prayers be answered? Some will, and some won't. Keep practicing. You will get more comfortable as time goes on. If you keep at it, one day it will become so much easier, and you may eventually do this for others. Then the power of Jesus' name will astound both you and them! It is faith building!

Just this last week as allergy season approached, I could feel a sneeze coming on and the itch begin. I focused on that itch, and told it to STOP, to GO, in the name of the Lord Jesus Christ. I told the enemy he wasn't going to get so much as a sneeze out of me. It receded. The allergy tried again and again. But each time, I told it to GO! We have to keep at it. Never give up, give in, or let the enemy steal the position of authority we have been given.

If we don't see the immediate results we are looking for, does that tarnish the name of God? No! Does it mean others don't have enough faith? No! Does it mean we don't have enough faith? No. We are called to pray. God is the One who answers in His timing and in His way. But if we don't ask, seek, and knock, we will miss so much of what God **does** want to do in and through our lives.

Always finish with thanks. Giving Jesus praise, glory, and honor!

NOTES:

14

SUMMARY AND PRAYERS

Mark 16:17

And these signs will accompany those who believe:
In my name they will drive out demons; they will speak in new tongues;

Summary

Step one: Start with repentance on your part. Confess all sins and come into agreement with God's Word. Receive His forgiveness.

Step two: Forgive those who have harmed you. This is a choice, not a feeling. Leave the feelings for God to help you with.

Step three: Restitution, if needed. Pay back whatever you might owe.

Step four: Ask the Holy Spirit to reveal the wound that needs healing today. Then ask for His healing in that area of your soul/body.

Step five: Identify any dark/unclean spirits associated with this wound. Tell them to GO in the name of Jesus Christ—their assignment is finished.

Step six: Breathe out the darkness. Breathe in the Holy Spirit.

Step seven: Give praise and thanks to Jesus Christ for all He has done to break the power of the devil in your life. Claim the promise of deliverance in the name of the Lord Jesus Christ.

Prayers

Prayer for Step One - Repentance:

Father, please forgive me for _____. I'm so very sorry. I agree with Your Word that speaks against this, and I choose to align my life and my thoughts with Your Truth.

Prayer for Step Two - Forgiveness:

I choose for forgive _____ for _____.

Prayer for Step Five - Identification:

I command the spirit of _____ to GET OUT in the name of the Lord Jesus Christ!!
You have no right to (Name) _____.
I am/they are a child of the living God.
You have to leave NOW! GO! GO! GO!

Simple Prayer for Physical Healing:

In the name of the Lord Jesus Christ, I command the pain in
_____ to GO!

Any infection, irritation, inflammation etc... GO NOW. In
Jesus' name.

You have no right to be here. (Name)_____ is a child of
the living God.

GET OUT! NOW!

Salvation and Freedom Prayer:

Father in Heaven,

I believe Your Son, Jesus, died on the Cross for my sins and
rose again from the dead. I confess all sins, known and
unknown, and I'm sorry for them. I renounce them all. I forgive
all others as I desire You to forgive me. Please forgive me now.
I thank You, Father, for the blood of Your Son, Jesus Christ,
which cleanses me from all sin. You redeemed me by Your
blood, and I now belong to You, and I want to live for You. I
come to You now as my Deliverer. You know my special needs,
the things that bind, that torment, that defile, and any unclean
spirit. I claim the promise of Your Word. *"Whosoever calls on
the name of the Lord Shall be delivered."* I call upon You now,
in the name of the Lord Jesus Christ. Deliver me and set me
free. Amen.

<u>Prayer for Inner Healing:</u>

(Close your eyes and have some time with God.)

Holy Spirit, bring a memory or memories to my mind that You want to heal today.

(The memories that come may hurt, but that pain is about to go. And if any spirit inflicted you on that day, taking you into bondage, it will be gotten rid of also.)

Father, I submit these memories to You and ask You to heal them. I am choosing to forgive, forget and to be healed, in Jesus' Name.

Thank You for healing these wounds.

Thank You that every spirit attached to them will go now, in the name of Jesus.

I tell all pain, frustration, fear, etc... Command whatever it is to Go! Now! In Jesus' name.

(See "Step Five" prayer.)

Jesus, You came to bind up the brokenhearted. That is what You are doing here today. You came to set the captives free. I am set free on this day, by the Great I AM! Thank You for releasing me from darkness. Never again can the enemy use this against me. I proclaim Your GOOD NEWS!

Thank You, and praise You, Lord Jesus!!

NOTES:

NOTES:

15

SCRIPTURE SUGGESTIONS

Nehemiah 8:10

Don't be dejected and sad, for the joy of the Lord is your strength.

Isaiah 42:10

Sing a new song to the Lord! Sing his praises from the ends of the earth.

Hebrews 4:12

For the word of God is alive and powerful! It is sharper than the sharpest two-edged sword cutting between soul and spirit, between joint and marrow.

Matthew 10:29-31

But not a single sparrow can fall to the ground without your Father knowing it. And the very hairs on your head are all numbered. So don't be afraid. You are more valuable to God than a whole flock of sparrows.

Joshua 1:9

I command you – be strong and courageous! Do not be afraid or discouraged. For the Lord your God is with you wherever you go.

Proverbs 28:1

The wicked run away when no one is chasing them, but the godly are as bold as lions.

Ephesians 6:18

Pray in the spirit at all times and on every occasion.

John 3:16

For God so loved the world that he gave his only Son that whoever believes in him should not perish but have eternal life.

Psalm 118:8

It is better to take refuge in the Lord than to trust in man.

Matthew 19:26

Humanly speaking it is impossible, but with God everything is possible.

Psalm 10:12

Arise, O Lord: Punish the wicked O God!

James 1:19

My dear brothers and sisters, be quick to listen, slow to speak, and slow to get angry.

Matthew 7:12

Do for others what you would like them to do for you.

Mark 16:17

And these signs will accompany those who believe: in my name they will drive out demons; they will speak in new tongues.

Joel 2:32

And everyone who calls on the name of the Lord will be saved; for on Mount Zion and in Jerusalem there will be deliverance, as the Lord has said...

1 Peter 2:24

He personally carried our sins in his body on the cross so that we can be dead to sin and live for what is right. By his wounds you are healed.

NOTES:

NOTES:

LEARN MORE ABOUT DIANE AT:
HTTP://DIANECSHORE.COM

FICTION BOOKS BY DIANE C. SHORE

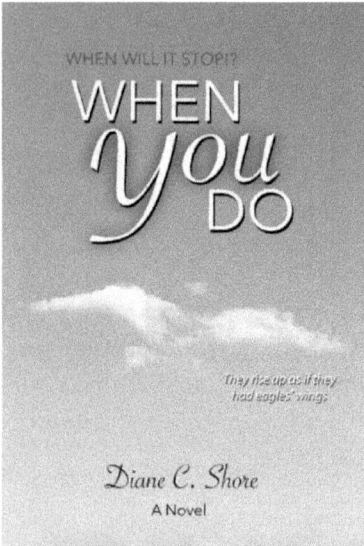

When YOU Do
ISBN: 978-0-123456789

ROSIE I
ISBN: 978-0990523192

ROSIE II
ISBN: 978-0-990523185

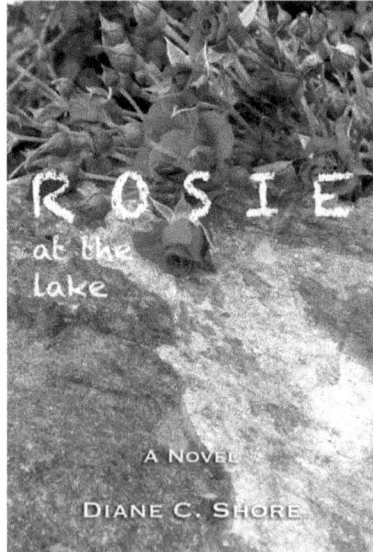

ROSIE III
ISBN: 978-1732678507

NON-FICTION BOOKS BY DIANE C. SHORE

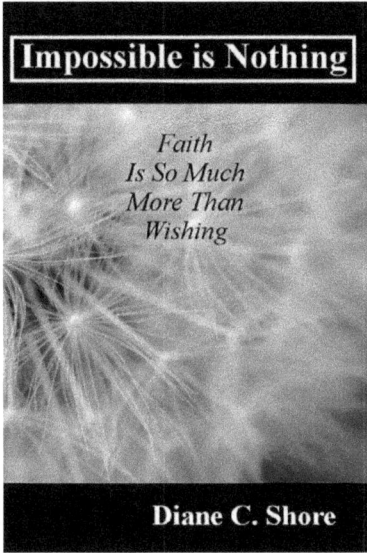

Impossible is Nothing

Faith Is So Much More Than Wishing

Diane C. Shore

ISBN: 978-0990523161

The SAND Room

Searching And Noticing the Divine

Volume I

Then Joseph stored up grain in great abundance like the sand of the sea, until he stopped measuring it, for it was beyond measure. Genesis 41:49 NASB

Diane C. Shore

ISBN: 978-0990523130

A true story of what Jesus can do with a broken heart.

It **STARTED** *in the* **DARK**

DIANE C. SHORE

Weeping may stay for the night...

ISBN: 978-0990523109

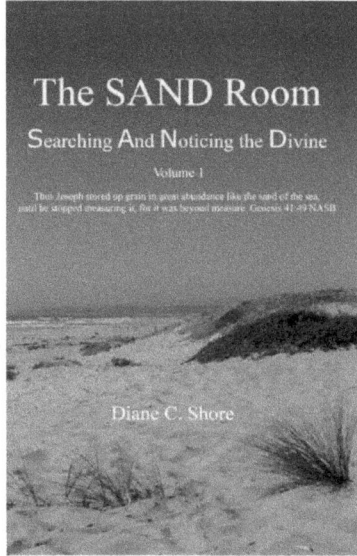

A true story of what Jesus can do with a broken heart.

It **ENDED** *in the* **LIGHT**

DIANE C. SHORE

Rejoicing comes in the morning!

ISBN: 978-0990523147

www.ingramcontent.com/pod-product-compliance
Lightning Source LLC
Chambersburg PA
CBHW071928020426
42331CB00010B/2776